Michael Wagner

Illustrated by Pablo Márquez

Rude Little Reggie is rude to everyone and everything. And he never learns his lesson.

Once, he was even rude at his very own pony party.

Reggie's mum had invited all of his friends to his party. Even Sam from next door.

But the most exciting thing was that she'd invited a pony called Fudge.

Reggie wanted the first ride, so he climbed onto Fudge's back.

"Give me a ride, NOW!" he demanded.

Fudge did not move. He just sat down and wriggled so that Reggie would slide off.

Reggie's friend, Augustus, scrambled onto Fudge's back and said, "Go, pony! Move!"

Fudge made Augustus slide off, too.

Reggie's other friends, April, May and June, also demanded rides. But Fudge would not budge for them either.

“You’re ruining my party!” Reggie said to Fudge.

Fudge didn’t seem to mind.

Just then, Sam came over.

"Wow!" he exclaimed. "You've got a pony. Can I please have a ride?"

"You can try," grumbled Reggie. "But silly old Fudge doesn't even move!"

“He makes you slide off,” said April.
“He doesn’t like children,” complained May.
“He won’t budge for anyone,” moaned June.

Sam climbed onto Fudge's back and asked, "Could I please have a ride, Fudge?"

Fudge nodded and happily trotted around the garden.

“That’s not fair,” exclaimed Reggie. “Why did Fudge give Sam a ride and not us?”

"I bet it's because Sam has brown hair," suggested May.

"But I have brown hair too!" said Reggie.

“I bet it’s because Sam has blue eyes,” said June.
“But I have blue eyes too!” said Augustus.

"I know!" exclaimed April. "I bet it's because Sam said please!"

Fudge and Sam finished their ride around the garden. Sam hopped down and helped April to climb on.

"Can I have a ride, PLEASE?" she asked.

Fudge trotted off.

“You just have to say please,” said Augustus. “That’s easy!”

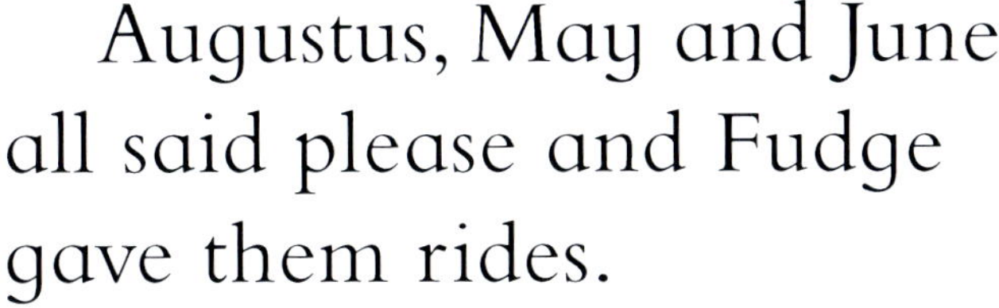

Augustus, May and June all said please and Fudge gave them rides.

Reggie didn't want to say please, but he wanted a ride. After all, it was his pony party.

He climbed onto Fudge's back and yelled, "Go, *donkey*! PLEASE!"

Fudge didn't budge.

"I said please!" cried Reggie. "That's not fair!"

Fudge looked around at Reggie for a moment, then snorted and took a step forward.

"At last!" said Reggie. "Go on! Get moving!"

Fudge did get moving.

He took off like a race horse. He sped around the garden. Reggie could hardly hold on!

He almost fell into the rose bush …

and the cactus plant.

On the last turn, Reggie could not hang on. He flew right off Fudge's back.

He landed on something brown that looked like mud … but it wasn't.

Splat!

Sitting in a pile of pony poo, Reggie had finally learnt his lesson …

… or had he?

"You stink, pony poo!" he said.